ECHO LOCATION
a guide to SEA POINT
for residents and visitors

KAREN PRESS

POETRY
Gecko

ECHO LOCATION
a guide to SEA POINT
for residents and visitors

KAREN PRESS

Welcome

in

Sea Point

First published in 1998 by Gecko Poetry
an imprint of Gecko Books
21 Hereward Road
Umbilo, Durban 4001, South Africa

Echo Location. A Guide to Sea Point for Residents and Visitors

ISBN 1-875011-21-8

Nothing in this book is true.

The completion of this work was assisted by a grant from
the Foundation for the Creative Arts.

The publisher acknowledges financial assistance for the publication of this work
from Buchu Books and the Arts and Culture Trust of the President

Book and cover design: Welma Odendaal

Cover illustration: Lien Botha

Set in Cochin by WO Editorial Design, PO Box 377, Green Point 8051

Printed by Kohler Carton and Print, Pinetown

Earlier versions of some of the poems in this collection
have appeared in *New Coin, New Contrast, Illuminations* and *West Coast Line*.

Acknowledgements
Xhosa translations on pages 32, 64 and 73 by Pamella Maseko.
Found poems and quotations from the following original sources:
Page 10: James Hamilton-Paterson, *Seven-Tenths. The Sea and Its Thresholds*
         Vintage 1993, page 101
Page 17: Commemorative plaque, Bantry Bay coastline
Page 18: Marischal Murray, *Under Lion's Head* AA Balkema 1964 pages 6-7
Page 21: Marischal Murray, *Under Lion's Head* AA Balkema 1964 page 94
Page 40: Marischal Murray, *Under Lion's Head* AA Balkema 1964 page 32
Page 48: *Style Decor Supplement* August 1995, *Atlantic Sun* (various editions),
         Cape Times (various editions)
Page 57: Uma Shashikant Mesthrie *The Tramway Road Removals, 1959-61* Institute for
         Historical Research and the Department of History Southern African and
         Contemporary History Seminar no. 17, 17 May 1994
Page 91: Quotations from *Robben Island*, an information brochure compiled by the SA
         Communications Service for the Department of Correctional Services, 92, and
         from the documentary film *Robben Island: Our University*, directed by Lindy Wilson.

Photographs courtesy of the South African Library (PHA), Diane Retief, Julia Martin,
the author.

Contents

Out here we are on the edge of
something: of drowning, fear,
understanding. The huge unseen city
itself seems always on the cusp of
vanishing, it is so delicate and its true
nature so elusive. It is a place whose
strangeness is far greater than we can
know even as we painstakingly try to
identify each snapping shrimp, each
grunting fish, the soft concussion –
like a cloth being flapped – of a
sizeable fish taking evasive action
somewhere nearby. But then we, too,
are stranger than we imagine. We
hang here, inquisitive carbon-based life
forms, knowing that every atom of
carbon now in our bodies was once in
the interior of a star. For an instant we
dissolve, are without form, become
nothing but the point at which the
three axes plotting this three-
dimensional borderland intersect.

James Hamilton-Paterson
Seven-Tenths. The Sea and Its
Thresholds

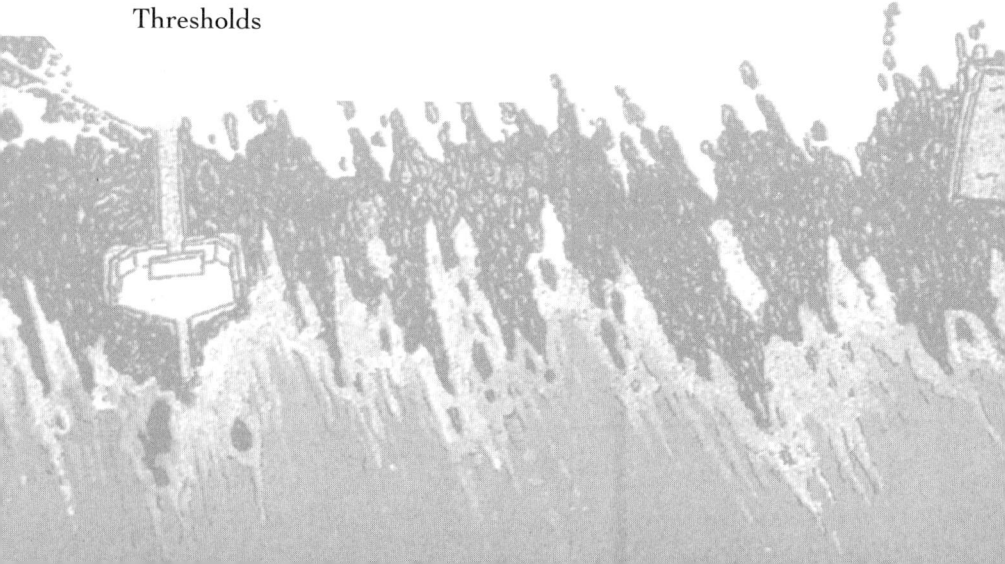

As our visitors from oversea and up-country to the 'Cape Beautiful,' will assuredly pay a visit to Sea Point, the following lines are penned in the hope that they may be an aid to those who come amongst us for the first time.

Sea Point stretches for four miles along the base of Signal Hill and Lion's Head, and derives its name from a rocky mass, on which during a gale the sea breaks with tremendous force. It prides itself on having a very much better climate than the other suburbs of Cape Town, due principally to a lesser rainfall, speedy drainage of surface water by abrupt slope of the mountains and proximity to the sea, and to the fact that the slopes are fully exposed to the rays of the afternoon sun. Another great point in its favour is the comparative immunity from the south-east summer gales.

The death-rate is exceedingly low, being on the average about 7 per 1000.

Tramps in & about the Peninsula (1908)

Prologue

Mesmerised
by a bead on a string
(and the string is a net
and the net falls over us
and) we lie there like silver fish
staring entranced at the smiling sky
that smells like sea, and it's so blue we forget
we're not breathing

in this tideless bowl of bliss,
dreamstruck

in the present tense that never leaves
the shadow of the old mantis
lifting the strings of the bikini top
in his slow claws, pulling them loose:

fresh bread of all countries rises like angels
in clouds of cinnamon sugar and olive oil,
hearts discover their many mouths sipping
the small boys in doorways, the tanned girls on corners,
and framed by driftwood limbs

the day swells like a downy peach
over whose sweet flesh a child rides a tricycle

gleefully round and round, spreading
the gold urine of an enormous dog

in spirals, wider and wider,
entranced by its sour shimmer.

WHEREVER LAND BEGINS

WHEREVER LAND BEGINS

water pearls on the old slate
walls grown out of the sand

drops cling to the black skin
tiny moons

rolling cheek to stone, cheek to sky
curious for the smell of sun

pressing their fingerprints in the cracks
the distance of centuries

reaching for something they remember
warming up, dozing off,
                        letting go

the sand smiles, shuffles in shyly
to drink, looking away, happy child with a secret

Sea Point is a gastronome's paradise. An introduction to its cuisine requires

CONTACT ZONE

THE ROCKS BETWEEN THIS PLAQUE
AND THE SEA
REVEAL AN IMPRESSIVE CONTACT ZONE
OF DARK SLATE WITH PALE
INTRUSIVE GRANITE.
THIS INTERESTING EXAMPLE OF
CONTACT BETWEEN
A SEDIMENTARY AND AN IGNEOUS ROCK
WAS FIRST RECORDED BY CLARKE ABEL
IN 1818.
SINCE ITS DISCOVERY IT HAS HAD
AN INSPIRING INFLUENCE ON THE
HISTORICAL DEVELOPMENT OF GEOLOGY.
NOTABLE AMONGST THOSE
WHO HAVE DESCRIBED IT
IS CHARLES DARWIN WHO VISITED IT IN 1836.

.

nothing more than an eager eye and an empty stomach. A seven-day eating plan is

RECREATION

found poem

In the later 1700s the social life of Cape Town
could hardly have been described as gay.

The Dutch themselves were well aware of boredom.
Headed by Martin Oloff Bergh, and Adriaan van Schoor
(a one-time Landdrost of Stellenbosch),
they petitioned the Governor, Ryk Tulbagh,
for a grant of land (about two acres)
where they could establish what today might be called
a Country Club.

The locality they favoured was –
in the language of their document –
achter de zoo genaamde Waterplaats, aan de voet des Leeuwenberges:
beyond the so-called Waterfront,
at the foot of the Lion Mountain.
In fact, at a corner of Sea Point.

On 22nd October 1766, the Council of Policy,
in conclave at the Castle, approved the petitioners' request,
'knowing that it cannot prejudice the interests of others'.

Some two acres of land were duly granted them,
on perpetual lease
but on the express condition that the place was to be
used for 'recreation' only.

offered here that will guide you through this 'world in one suburb', but don't resist

On the site was a spring of fresh water,
and the petitioners were granted the sole use of this
'inasmuch as slaves and miscreants are wont
to befoul the place by watering cattle there'.

Their petition duly granted, the promoters proceeded
to erect a building on the site,
and by the middle of 1767
the country club was in full swing.

temptations that detour from this map. Those of a systematic temperament may

19TH CENTURY GRATITUDE

Sea captains come to anchor here,
unloading fattened dreams of dark barbarity,
shaking the crumbs of insignificance from their beards.

Their wives unearth the tranquil soil,
plant children, servants and the pincers of God's charity.
Leopards and forests are turned away.

The lion's rump, bought from a guttural horseman,
is sliced into parlour views and roses.
Natives are covered with cloth and kept moving.

Municipal power fills each tobacco pouch.
The sea seems to have learnt placidity.
Fog rises only at night, pacing the sand in silence.

Ships founder visibly on the rocks.
The captains frown at the drowning cries
their grandchildren collect in candy-striped sunhats.

Should they be thanking someone?
The wind blows in from Gallows Hill,
reminding them to relax.

Dark hands wheel their Bath chairs along.
Their wives exchange recipes for wreaths.
The sun peels their skin.

work their way through the cuisine of every country, from British roast beef to Thai

INDECENTLY HILARIOUS

found poem

At 11.16 pm on 16th April, 1929,
the last train for Sea Point
pulled out from Monument Station.

The *Argus* published a full 'Obituary',
describing how more than 1,200 people,
some of them indecently hilarious,
crowded into the Funeral Train, which, for this occasion,
was not driven by brash electric power
but was decorously hauled by an old steam engine.

At the Sea Point terminus a wreath was hung
in memory of the Sea Point Line.
Along the Beach Road crowds waved farewell.
At one station a funeral pyre was kindled,
consuming posters, railway timetables and
a signalman's flag.

At 12.15 a.m., the last Sea Point train of all disappeared
into the darkness of the railway yards.

Next morning, labourers from Langa and Ndabeni
arrived at the station, bewildered to find no train
to take them to their work at Sea Point.

coconut and lemon grass curry, via Israeli humus, Indian biryani, Portuguese

PURPLE

You won't remember, but I can tell you.
Purple came to Sea Point in December 1968
when my cousin Ronnie and her best friend Tamara
came back from their Musgrove & Watson tour
through Europe's eight capitals and London in six weeks
wearing clothes from Carnaby Street.

Lilac ribbed sweaters showing the exact size of their busts.
Mauve patent leather belts clutching their waists.
Calf-length aubergine skirts.
Lavender tights. Mulberry boots.
Plum melton jackets and violet velvet floppy hats.
It was 30°C and they looked ready to faint.
My aunts couldn't stop telling each other
how purple they were.

They took their sugarplum lips and eyelids
down to the beachfront, their foreign psychedelic dresses
creeping higher up their legs with each paving step
away from home, and leaned against
the boys in their bulging jeans on the rail, pretending
they weren't virgins and knew what caused
the acid green and orange colours they were wearing.
Purple was as good as sex in 1968
for my grown-up Sea Point cousins
from good homes.

Jou ma se poes!
Walk the dog. Walk
the bladdy dog.
Jou piss poes! piss
poes! jou – jou –

Ek sal jou fokken naai!
Jou naai! Ja, jy! Jy!
Moenie wegloop nie!
Jou naai!

cabalkau and Provençal onion soup. Even African cuisine can be reconstructed by

IN THOSE DAYS

we were exempt from politics
Politics
what we represented was

summer
ice creams
Sunday walks on the beachfront before lunch

the very poor never envied our flats,
our cockroaches, our rats;
the very rich owned them

we fought battles
over dustbins, maids' rooms, prostitutes

nobody wanted to organise for or against us
we didn't own the sea
so no-one could claim it back

our corruption stretched no further
than the servants' quarters

now things are different

there are people among us who live like kings:
our children and their architects
trading in futures

they sunbathe all day as if they want to look good
in the news footage from the war front

those in self-catering accommodation, using supplies from one of the local

SINGLE PASSAGE

The old men
had not expected to be abandoned.

Striding alone on the patterned stones
spattered with sea scum like foamy brains
they experimented with being
young again, at the edge of a new home

and found it didn't work.
They were old, and had never learnt
to be sentimental about landscape.

They had the choice of playing cards
with each other, arguing about politics
or folding silently inside a nurse's shadow.

Just ships some gene was using
to get from Vilnius to Perth. You could see
the thought flickering in their eyes:
bloody long detour.

supermarkets. And the most idiosyncratic tastes are catered for: whether you adore

THE FIRST THIRTY-SEVEN YEARS

We were just camping out.
I put up a wall
and my mother bought carpets.
There was a door for the sea.

My father stood dropping anchor
year by year. I watched him lowering the rope,
he was swaying with a faraway look
and he said he loved me, lowering the rope.

My brother kicked a ball around a lot
and I was reading. I never knew
he broke his heart young.
I buried mine in a wave.

My father died. My mother went home.
My brother was away somewhere, walking.
I moved to the other side of the wall,
just camping out.

The sea could come in my sleep, or the wind.
I've no rope, my father left no rope.

masked butternut or marinated squid, you'll find it in small, medium and

RECORDED HISTORY

(extracts from the catalogue of the South African Library)

economy-size takeaway portions on the streets of Sea Point. Day 1 Quintessentially

What naches?
You give your kids everything,
and then they turn round and do this to you.
A schoch she's living with. Here in Fresnaye.

Sea Point Breakfast at the New York Deli: Cappuccino buttered bagel with

RUST FLAKES ON THE TONGUE

(a myth of origins)

100% SILK

Alida's not my name.
It's from a dress left on the beach.
Alida Creations. 100% Silk.

(He must have carried her away wrapped in his arms,
in his towel. For her to have left that dress behind.
She must have been in love.)

I had to dirty it before I could wear it,
in case she came back and saw me.
Silk doesn't last; I ended up using it to wash cars.
But I kept the name.

They hate me washing cars. Want me to use my body
to earn money. 'Woman's advantage.'
I tell them here in Sea Point there's more would pay
for their cocks than my cunt. Berger broke my teeth for that.
Called me 'seekoei'. 'Kooi.'
Everyone laughed, till I stabbed him with a bottle.
Piece of shit. I won't let anyone touch me.

When my milk was still coming, I drank it myself.
He threatened to tell about the baby. So what?

My mother came all the way to Sea Point
to point at buildings and accuse.
A story about murders. I try never to see her.

She took my hand even though it was dirty.
Ma, Ma, don't expect anything from me. It hurts so.
I'm a piece of rubbish. 100%.

cheddar cheese and rocket or smoked salmon and cream cheese, chocolate

ROTTEN FISH

Law and order isn't easy.
Anyone can lay a charge.
The door of the police station is always open.

Sergeant Oliphant (unaware
he's descended from a long line of Ndlovus
with other, ongoing concerns)
has no reason to believe he should believe
a woman who smells and drips sand,
accusing unknown people of murdering
other unknown people.

He scratches his head.
'Salt water cures lice,' Alida says.

Anyone is capable, Sergeant Ndlovu tells himself.
Shall I arrest every person on the beach
who has refused this woman something?
Murder is a cloudy thought.

Sergeant Oliphant would like very much
not to make a dangerous mistake.
He knows that law and order
is just a thin umbrella sold by those who pour the rain.

'Get out of here,' he says.
'You smell like rotten fish.'

croissant. Lunch at the Hard Rock Café: Nachos, guacamole, chili dip and chips,

PROBABILITY

She was so angry about rotten fish,
she decided to believe her mother.
After all those years.

Zikwezaa zindlu. Izidumbu kwezaa zindlu.
A fairy tale, a croon, a lullaby.

Akuziva wena? Oho ebhusuku ziyakhala, ziyakhala.
A misty cry of birds along the promenade.

Ndizibonile zonke. Ndibabukele besifa. Ndide ndiphuphe nongazo.
An old voice muttering in an empty room.

'Tell me why it couldn't have happened –
I, standing in some stolen dress on a bed of dead shells,
tell me why my mother didn't see what she saw.
What dirt was she cleaning away, day after day after day
from the groin and armpits of this place?
All the years of her life,
all the sobbing ghosts she poured into my lap,
why shouldn't I offer them to you now?
Something of my mother's, to worry about.

'Have you seen a whale rotting on the beach?
It stays and stays. Every bit of it.'

Mexican beer. Dinner at San Marco: Carpaccio, baby calamari sautéed in garlic

KLIP IN DIE BOS

Come down to the beach in the silver night
when sea-dew covers the railings like cold
sweat and the blue shells soften their wiry beards
in Alida's hands. Throw shadows near the wall
so that she can work safely in darkness, away
from the men who claim all rights to the sandy gallery
where they display shell crocodiles and hearts
for loose change. Alida makes fish leaping
between child skulls with yellow hibiscus blossoms
in their mouths, tango dancers
in a cemetery around a waiting space,
blank paper or a grave.
Near dawn, she weaves a birdtailed script across it
with kelp fronds torn from their fat stems,
and sprinkles spirits in their curls,
and as the sky begins to pale she throws a match.

Move away, now that the joggers are stopping,
panting like lycra dolphins,
escape the dogwalkers tottering in tangled leads,
the poodles backing away from the flaming message:
        Look for death
        in your homes
        Sea Point.
Someone is looking around for a police patrol.

Leave. You don't need to get involved in this.
You don't live here.

butter, litchi, mango and strawberry fruit sorbets. SPECIAL OFFER Buy two

WRONGFUL DEATH

(A case study)

Morry lived a quiet life.
His children in Australia,
his wife dead seven years.

Mornings on the beachfront
around dawn, he walks, talking to the other widowers
of grandchildren and crime and doctors' bills.
On his way home he buys a roll, perhaps the paper.
Saves his teabag for a third cup.
Does the crossword, plays cards with the TV on,
waiting for the sport.

Imagine Morry being accused of murder.

It happened. One day there was a knock
at the door: two policemen wanting to search
for dead bodies in his flat.
One watched him while the other opened his cupboards,
unmade the bed. They wouldn't tell him anything.

They were already out the door
when they heard a noise. In the bathroom
Morry was turning blue, groping along the floor
for his pills, falling.

They radioed for an ambulance
but there was really no point.

frozen braai packs and get a free bottle of braai marinade only at our Regent Road

TRUTH

SOME OF THE NAMES found burning in the dawn sand at Broken Bath:

Rapallo
Knightsbridge
Normanhurst
Lisdale
Villa Rosa
Quendon Mansions

The morning air was wild with tension

hot white silence of the named, shivering
laughter of the untouched.
Some threw coins down on the square rag.
Others cursed or tried to punch them
for their gloating generosity.
Dogs ran howling from the kelp
their owners threw for them.

ALIDA EATS BREAKFAST EVERY DAY

The tide changes with the moon

Someone came deep in the night
with a R10 note and a name
to commit to memory, then burn.
The next night someone
repaid him in kind.
Alida saw the future. Soon
she was on a roll.

Old man dies after police visit

Days later bones emerged
in a bathroom wall due
for dampproofing.
The buildings held their breath
while police and councillors
sucked in the winds
of trends and implications
and spat out a policy.

New source of foreign exchange

Trucks roared along the sand
collecting the kelp
for export to Japan.

Alida opens a building society account

RECONCILIATION

Maids and caretakers stand to one side, arms folded,
no idea which way the wind is blowing for them
as police vans drive around collecting bones and bits of wall,
fingerprinting sixty-year-old brickwork.
Men in silk shawls and black cassocks come to pray
over carriers of rubble.

And then, the way the berg wind breaks and sweet rain
washes all the dust away, the air shakes itself loose of history
and laughs.

'What's worse than finding a body in your cupboard?
– Finding half a body.' Schoolboys swop skeleton stories.
Their parents exchange names of contractors, bricklayers, plasterers,
painters, dampproofers, architects, surveyors, roofers, rubble removers,
landscapers, designers, tilers, cabinetmakers.

It is the season of renovations.
Open plan.
Waterproof injection.
Aluminium frames.
Louvre shutters.
Pastel mouldings.
Look, we have come through!

The maids and caretakers return to their old,
unexcavated warrens,
or stand on corners, comparing quantities of rubble.
It never stops.

milkshakes, eggs, bacon, hash browns and free plastic object. Lunch at the

ORIGINAL DARK

Strangers to freedom, in ghostly silence
they tried out the tender pavements,
sculpting the night smells into doorways.

Stretching tentatively
like convalescents, like cats
licking the sea air, arching
their memories, shaking off
the grit bandages of time

they rubbed against beachfront benches,
establishing their borders, then drifted
up the hill into the private avenues of their biographies.

❊

Waking at night you feel
a new thickness in the air
like someone's breath on the pillow beside you,

an open-throated rush of dark
descending: there, at the very bottom
of the chasm a tiny skeleton

stirring, looking up,
reassembling itself,
climbing out.

Rust flakes on the tongue
are a symptom.

Chicken Bar: Spitroast chicken pieces, hot chips, jelly and custard in separate tubs,

A MOST DESIRABLE LOCATION

A MOST DESIRABLE LOCATION

found poem

In this year of 1839
auctioneers selling properties
within the new Municipality
stressed points such as
'the avidity with which ground is sought for
in this interesting neighbourhood …
None of the lower classes of the population
either coloured or white,
reside within the limits of the Municipality
except those in service and residing
with the several proprietors.

'*There are no Canteens* within this Municipality:
the crimes of drunkenness and theft are of more rare
occurrence than in any other district of the Colony.

'No licence can be granted to any person
to sell by retail, wines spirituous or malt liquors,
spruce or ginger beer,
without the consent of three-quarters of the proprietors
residing within half a mile of the premises.

'Mosquitoes are unknown and
owing to its well-ventilated and airy situation
there are fewer flies than anywhere else
in the vicinity of Cape Town …'

buy some extra pickled onions at the till, Fanta or guava juice. Dinner at St

In flight
    the gulls shoot arrow cries
    across the night, lost hunters
calling
    torches flaring and fading,
soundings
    falling through darkness.

Elmo's: Very cheesy pizzas, Greek salad, ice cream and hot chocolate sauce,

Rules Binding on All Owners and Residents

1. Overcrowding is strictly forbidden. The maximum number of occupants per unit at any time must not exceed 4 persons (including children). The unit must be kept clean and free of vermin.

2. All refuse should be securely wrapped or put in paper bags and deposited in the bin in the lane at the rear of the building. Under no circumstances must rubbish, dirt, cigarette butts or boxes, chocolate papers, food scraps, odd bits of paper etc be deposited or thrown about the premises, particularly in the garden.

3. Washing must not be visible above the balcony parapet.

4. To maintain the respectability of the premises, windows should be covered with suitable curtaining (with white or cream lining) or blinds. Makeshift coverings as curtains will not be permitted.

5. Noise must be kept to a minimum and includes, inter alia, radios, videos, TVs, cars, children, animals and parties, particularly at night. No sound production (musical or otherwise) shall be made between the hours of 2pm and 4pm daily and between 11pm and 7am.

6. The keeping of animals (including reptiles and birds) in flats is officially forbidden. Any non-action by Trustees at any time against the keeping of domestic pets must not be construed as creating a precedent. Such animals must not be allowed to become a nuisance i.e. excessive barking of dogs, screeching of cats and general vicious behaviour, excreting on footpaths, steps or among plants, digging up, jumping on or breaking the plants.

Coke. Or find another kind of family atmosphere at the Pizzeria, where the veal

7. Residents are asked to ensure that their taps are FULLY turned off when not in use. Even a slow drip over a period of time can cause serious problems.

8. The owner of any unit, or the resident, shall not place or do anything on any part of the common property, including balconies, stoeps and gardens, which in the opinion of the Trustees is aesthetically displeasing or undesirable when viewed from outside. Furthermore, windows should be kept clean. Canopies and awnings must be of a style and colour sanctioned by the Trustees.

9. The utilisation of a unit for any unlawful practice, e.g. gambling, running a brothel or any other immoral sex activity, dealing in prohibited drugs, illicit diamond dealing or running an undesirable club, etc. will result in strong action by the Trustees, and the police will be informed.

10. No unit may be used as a storeroom and under no circumstances may dangerous or inflammable goods be stored in a flat.

Owners are reminded that the Trustees have the right to check on any unit if they have cause to suspect infringement of any of these rules, and they must be granted entrance to the flat for examination thereof when called upon to do so.

marsala and the mural of Naples Bay will keep you transfixed all evening. Stop!

MOONLIGHT IN TURD CITY

There was moonlight in Turd City
as the dogs dragged their bones along
and an ant on a garlic pita
inhaled and burst into song.

> *Oh where is my love, my Thea,*
> *my bearer of stalk and crumb?*
> *I lost my way in a black bag*
> *and when I escaped she was gone.*

He paused as a passing pigeon
dislodged a wet chip from the pile
blocking the overflow drainpipe,
and managed a wistful smile.

> *Tonight would have been our moment*
> *to settle and build a home.*
> *I've found her the perfect shelter:*
> *a hill bright as honeycomb.*

A gull with its beak full of sardines
spat feathery fins on the tar
and shrieked as its feet kicked the pita
and ant at the wheel of a car.

> *It steamed like a Christmas pudding;*
> *its softness was balm to my feet.*
> *The crenellations on its summit*
> *promised a safe retreat.*

Have you tried our kneidlach? Made on the premises with genuine Israeli matzo

The ant shrank away from a shadow
that scuttled enormously by;
his voice rose with such throbbing anguish
it plucked at the heart of a fly.

 What is my life without Thea?
 The spit of some god up above.
 Without her I'm flesh without spirit.
 Oh Thea, where are you, my love?

The ant did not know what the fly did:
that Thea, asleep on a paw,
had drowned when it splashed through a puddle
to swat at a roach on a door.

 'Oh ant, we are doomed!' the fly answered.
 'This world has no mercy on us.
 As small as we are, we're excluded
 from sharing its least speck of dust.'

The moon paused between two high walls
as the ant stepped in front of a foot,
then drifted away past a dog turd
squashed flat in the shape of a boot.

meal. Day 3 Detox day Breakfast on the beach: Sweetmelon sprinkled with

EXOTIC ENTERTAINMENT 1

Ever in touch with the market for pleasure
we can now offer a new entertainment:
Juanita, the woman whose breasts offer hits
of the purest cocaine in a soluble form.

Just one suck of her tumescent nipple
and you could be flying inside your own skin.
No more concern about how long it takes
for your erection to tune into your nostrils:
Juanita's milky treats are guaranteed to spread desire
through your stomach lining to all parts of your anatomy
simultaneously, ensuring that even your horny toes
and your bald brain will come together in ecstasy.

Choose your time, choose your nipple:
Juanita would love to drive you wild.

Sunday Special!
Add your name to the hat and you could receive
three free sucks in our lucky draw.

Note:
♥   Special discounts available for frequent users.
♥   All visits cash, payable in advance.
♥   Management not liable for clients' failure to achieve
     full satisfaction.
♥   Right of admission reserved.

cinnamon and lemon juice, ruby grapefruit juice mixed with sparkling mineral

EXOTIC ENTERTAINMENT 2

Tired of over-priced, over-used sources
of substances that leave you
Out of Control?

Then you should Come Home to Mama,
the mellow lady with the mellow taste.

Experience the soft, warm juices
of indigenous Cape dagga, straight
from the breasts that nourished a continent.

Spend an hour nestled
in Mama Afrika's arms,
drinking your cares away,
and fly out on a cloud of peace.

All health regulations stringently adhered to.
Group bookings by arrangement with management.
Muffins and rizlas also available.

water. Lunch from Nature's Best: Packet of mixed sprouts, chunk of tofu, spinach

THE RDP COMES TO SEA POINT

Dreams Do Come True

THE HOUSE, situated in Upper Fresnaye, on 550 square metres of prime real estate right under the mountain, has an astonishing vista stretching from Bantry Bay through to Green Point, taking in Robben Island and Saldanha Bay. Contemplating the sensational patterns of light and shade filtering through the glass gaps in the floating roof, while listening to the owner talk about his architectural vision for his dream home, is an exquisite escape from the everyday world.

New Abuse for Drain Covers

THE SCRAP METAL value of drain and manhole covers is not the only reason why thieves find them attractive. One reader phoned to tell me that drain covers were used twice to smash the front window of her car. Her warning to motorists is 'don't park near manholes or drain covers.'

New Gay Club for Sea Point

THE INLINE GAY CLUB is the first upmarket gay club to open in Sea Point. Offering various relaxation facilities from jacuzzis and steam baths to body rubs, showers and adult entertainment videos, the club is opened 24 hours on weekends and from 5pm until late on weekdays.

Entrance is by membership only and the reception will take all enquiries.

Build a faraway hostel for street people and take fear away from us

IS THE council waiting for a more serious tragedy than another mugging of an elderly Sea Point woman to take place before it makes a positive decision on removing the vagrants/street children from Three Anchor Bay?

It's quite obvious that all the vagrants are not using the night shelters by the mere fact that they are found loitering on the steps of blocks of flats – very often drunk!

The street children are no little angels, they sleep in undercover parking bays, break into cars and accost people coming to their cars at night. They intimidate caretakes and calling the police has proved fruitless.

I endorse the kibbutz system. Build a hostel on some land out of the city, appoint people with the right know-how to assist them to become self-sufficient, for example by growing vegetables or learning a trade. Install a television and issue a soccer ball for recreation!

EMPLOYMENT WANTED

Char – 4 days. Good refs. Alice 631 2489
Char – willing to work for accom. Phone 29-1456 after 5 pm.
Char – Honest and reliable, available 3 days – phone employer 99-4272.
Gardener – intelligent, experienced, available 3 days per week. Phone 29-6253.

'RDP ONLY FOR THOSE WHO PAY' – Nelson Mandela

muffin. Dinner at Alexander's: Bowl of mixed salad greens with balsamic vinegar

THE CARETAKER

The caretaker wears blue overalls
and has a name like John or Klaas.
He collects dirt and puts it out on the street.
He sweeps the passages and steps.
He waters the flowerbeds around the building.
He lives somewhere at the back.
You will know him when you see him.

and olive oil, marinated peppers and mushrooms, Mediterranean fruit platter.

THE FAIREST CAPE

the mountain only occasionally offers mothering
when the clouds remind it of cradles, mostly
it's being a landscape for German cheesemakers
cutting holes in itself to fit Carrara marble stakes
sucking in Nordic chrome tubes to press its water out

water sweet water
the children peed on their way to manhood

but the rocks here, patient as hospice nuns,
will hold any amount of palace weight
(sensitive, though, to the slightest scrape
of bare feet, twitching them off)
stones of every colour piled within lilac walls
of dreams imported duty-free, shingles so delicate
the nerve ends of the lion's breast don't mind
the pain, Spanish plaster covering fresh wounds
or the newest coral and rose mounting each other
in storeys paid for with hope

ghosts who pass are careful to imitate jasmine or servants,
not wanting to frighten the newcomers

you could cut conversations in half here, in quarters,
and spread them on different biscuits, they would taste
of the same salt and sour metal
we are all in this place because somewhere else
sadness and money converged

Halaal and Kosher pizzas delivered to your door, also Thai and Chinese takeaways.

speculators, trading journeys for wine
and a sunset so glorious we believe paradise
is some sailor's legend invented for a northern prince
who had not passed this coast one summer evening

heaven is beauty, not contentment,
we say, straining the liquor through our tongues,
eyeing the slope under the lion's ribs
where the shaft will be sunk,
waiting for dinner to appear

Glimpses of Women in Overalls

live-in

tin gives you no time, only
everything too hot, the taste of your own burnt tongue
immediately going cold, coagulation of fat on the palate

they say china holds the warmth,
allowing incredible flavours to seep like perfume
through the soft, moist cells that glow with pleasure
behind closed lips

off duty

like children, fearing any moment
the door bursting open:
why did you
where is my
who said you

one of the family

shadow
moving quietly along the world's outline
sharpening the brilliance of its whirling blades –
the keys, the voices, dancing, dust-free

yet somehow a stranger

bridge on heavy legs,
the strong right arm supporting
untold numbers of children and their parents,
maltese poodles, hot water cylinders, supermarkets, lavatories
the other jointed like a cracked wing,

Bauernfrükstück, pot of coffee with cream, fresh rolls, marmalade and honey. Or

reaching into the mist, as far as the eye can see
along its length pigeons building nest after nest,
the soft-throated rumbling of their incomprehensible songs
barely audible

get it cheaper across the road at the Vienna Coffee Shop; they buy their bread from

BALLAD OF THE SMALL BOYS AT SUNSET

Dusk opens its diamond-studded fan
over the beach. Last mothers shepherd their saltspun children
up the steps. Surfers lope into the shadows of their fins,
the last daylight clinging to their hair.

Behind the public toilets a rapist drinks himself to sleep.
Two men lean on the rail above the empty, floodlit pool
waiting for a signal to inch closer. A siren wails languidly.
The tender moon sinks back behind the hill.

From nowhere come the skinny boys to gather on the sand,
squabbling edgily until the smell of dreams wraps them in its viscous breath.
Inside each one a small darkness begins
to pulse, a grin bubbles and breaks, foam sliding across rocks.

Morning will find them tangled like a many-hearted beast
inside their crusted eyes, hands clasped over their hardened loins.

Zerbans anyway. Lunch at Europa: Avocado ritz, linefish of the day with tartare

TREATMENT

Hop, hop, two squares on,
one square off. Broken corners
cut the skin. The doctor comes
with needles. Lift your skirt.
Already? Is there something
that doesn't hurt?

From the window high up
I can see surfers far out there.
Their gold hair cresting
the tiny black waves.

Where are all the girls?
Can I go now?

sauce, fruit salad and ice cream. Dinner at La Perla: Snails in butter, seafood paella

If you want to know

Mortality
the one with the satin shoes
tripped down St. John's Road this morning
leaving a whole lot of children wailing.

Then Virtue
which had its own reward tucked in an inside pocket
arrived on the scene and rounded up everyone
in a chorus of street directions.
Chocolate, vanilla and mint crisp were the favourite promises.

Overhead was the sound of glass cracking
and a grey cloth billowed from a third-floor window.
The smell of fallen peaches was very strong
until Eternity in its dusty pants came and swept everything away.

or crayfish costing the same as a small pied à terre in Knightsbridge, cassata, Irish

HERE WE GO AGAIN

found poem
for the pupils of Kings Road Primary School
who were instructed to stay away from Tramway Road
but never told why

1. In 1953 it was estimated that there were 55 coloured families (142 adults and 126 children) and 3 Indian families (7 adults and 11 children) in Tramway Road and the adjoining Ilford Street.

2. Most of the residents had lived in the area for most of their lives.

3. The children of these families attended the Tramway Road Coloured Primary School.

4. Proclamation 190 of 1957.

5. In November 1959, a few months after the expiry of the evacuation date, Frederick Johannes Mitchell, a 58-year-old resident of Tramway Road, was found hanging from a tree ... His wife, Helene Catriena, said that because he had to look for alternative accommodation he had lost weight, suffered from insomnia and had become a recluse.

6. Florence Wepener tried to sound cheerful about her new home in Bonteheuwel. She was hoping to get some grass from Sea Point and develop her garden.

7. Frances Jacobs made a point of visiting her home in Sea Point every week. She sat on the stoep and just cried each time.

coffee. Or go for a more homely feel at the Wooden Shoe, the oldest steakhouse in

8. As for the road they vacated, by November 1961 the press reported that it had become 'a ghost road'. It also became 'a road of fear' as drunks, vagrants and squatters moved in.

9. The Cape Town City Council bought most of the cottages in Tramway Road and planned to demolish the homes and establish a playground there.

10. Today the land remains municipal property.

Sea Point, with a cosy Swiss atmosphere. Day 5 Rediscovering roots Breakfast in

GREEN TIN

Green as new wheat
the landfill lawns grow
over bone and paper
and the dust that remains
after decades of rotting
have settled the soil
that was skin and muscle,
eyes and nipples.

Far below, safely concealed
from small bare feet,
tin still rusts;
as the boys play soccer
broken bottles cut each other
and the lava crusts split open
each time prams bounce
over hard lumps in the grass.

Africa: (Ask a domestic worker to share her breakfast with you - offer a small

TIPS FOR VISITORS

Eat slowly and sip water frequently.

Close envelopes with extra glue.

Everything warms up.

The thin small angular men with low-slung pants are the dangerous ones.

You need never be satisfied with yesterday's bread.

Ask at any corner café for doctors, dentists, vets, physiotherapists, manicurists, hairdressers, dieticians or psychologists in your vicinity.

Carry your keys in a separate pocket.

The mist is clean and good for your skin.

Small bushes at ground level contain rats.

Don't visit the library if you're in a hurry.

There are tiny green parks on many corners.

People shouting are not calling you.

Fresh water is available in all public toilets.

Never sit alone in a park.

All pharmacies sell chocolates.

Halaal food is safer.

On hot evenings big things fly through windows.

Count your change.

payment.) Mieliepap with butter and jam, chicory/coffee mix. Lunch in the

CHILDREN'S CORNER

Rehearsal

The town hall shimmered in the sun, a mint green sugar palace.
Through the door we stepped into shadows,
their long fingers pointing towards silence.

We clustered in corners in a cold room
half-costumed, our pink satin shoes
drawing spirals in old dust.

The piano was hard and impatient, a stranger shouting.
We formed our circle, hugging each other's shoulders,
touching the goose bumps, giggling.

Our mothers shook their heads crossly and we felt better.
Then a lady wheeled her daughter in,
a girl our age, with long hair and a rug on her legs.

The piano paused. Our teacher counted the beat.
Outside a bottle broke and a child shouted:
'Take me to the *beach*!'

She was dying, and we danced without looking at her
but her eyes followed us everywhere: dark pools
like the stage we were practising to leap across.

Uthe umntwana angahlala ngamaxesha
esikolo, qha angangeni ebesini.

Lithuanian ambience of any delicatessen: Chopped herring or liver, gherkins,

THE ILIAD (CONT.)

Gerald, aged four years, eyed the rat with venom.
It had a tail for chopping off, which was good.
It seemed to like his fallen sandwich, which was bad.
The teacher called him back inside.
Tomorrow he would pounce.

The rat had children to feed, and stored
the memory of Gerald at mid-morning dropping bread.
At dusk she went down the alley to fetch her brood
and settled them in a new nest behind the see-saw
at the bottom of the garden. The future looked bright.

Achilles had Paris.
Dingaan had Pretorius.
Gerald will have the rat.
The rat will have Gerald.

The rat will win, in a general sense.

History will show
one less property developer,
one more small corpse with tooth marks on its chubby palm,
a sudden upsurge in pest control in 1995.
The rat's tail, emerging from Gerald's fist
like an aerial on a portable radio,
will be preserved in a forensic laboratory
until the space is needed, issuing no warnings.

potato salad, rye bread. Dinner in the Orient: Chili bites, lassi, Malaysian stirfry

CRIMES OF LOVE

It could have happened to anyone in that income bracket.
Very few parents of their generation know
what their children get up to.
And it has to be said, she was a good daughter
in all the ways that count.

Their grief made them behave very badly.
(Apart from lying to the police, which was understandable.)

Many wondered, in fact, if they weren't in on it all the time.
All those luxury holidays, the penthouse like an art gallery.
Where did they think it came from? She was a single girl.
Leaving the country was never going to solve anything;
people want their money back, regardless.

You'd think in a building like that someone would hear something.
Neighbours always have an idea what's going on.
And there's a nightwatchman
but they say he was part of the deal.
Five million rands' worth of Bacons and Moores
taken without a sound is quite hard to believe.
Of course the insurance won't pay a cent yet.

And now she's dead, apparently. Perhaps it's for the best.
They shut the door on us when we went to condole;
they're telling everyone we're to blame
for enjoying her parties. They've been seen
at auctions, buying thirties' lithographs.
It must be hard to live with all the blank walls.
Art was always so much a part of their lives.

Indonesian Rijstafel, sweet and sour chicken, bow ties, ice cream and hot

GUESS WHO

Watch out where you're walking,
the late afternoon sweat with the sky ripening –
Oupa Schaapje's the kind one, you can take a sip
of whatever he offers, brushing sweetly past you,
but watch for Oupa Boeli, he has a mind for viciousness.

There have to be both of them or it doesn't work.

Grandfathers, light and dark.
They've been here all the time,
waiting for you. You have to be willing
to let yourself be kissed by invisible lips,
to unfold yourself on the lawn
while a truck hoots and seagulls with second sight
are laughing at you. Take it in good spirit.

For us, the world gets better.
We have passed the time of decay
and are unwrapping new skin for our century of happiness.
Come Oupa Schaapje and Oupa Boeli,
you must be here
to smell the fresh bread of the early mornings,
there's enough for you, more than enough. I will adopt you.

To live in the place where your grandfathers lived.
Imagine.

chocolate sauce. Weekend special: Apple Danish half-price, Norwegian salmon

Twinkle twinkle little star

imagine you are a point without dimensions
floating at a position K in space-time

and a little girl is running behind you
pushing you as you float off the edge
into the thermals that will carry you
along the axes of your space-time continuum

now
imagine a rope is attached to your axes
a rope held by a hypothetical hand
floating on another set of axes
outside your system of co-ordinates
carrying you along on another set of axes
outside your system of co-ordinates

relative to yourself you are quite still
and the rest of the universe is moving away
everyone is moving away
so you know you are dying or they are dying

all the time the little girl keeps pushing the space
that you are flying in and you move
further and further away as she gets closer
to the edge where the thermals will fetch her
when whoever is running behind her
pushes

less a third. German spoken here. Day 6 Budget special Street eats are plentiful

Did you see his eyes?
I swear, if he asks me out I'll just die. Is it true
he's the one in the Coke ad? My folks will kill me
but I don't care. I hear he takes girls
to Llandudno and they do it behind the rocks,
with wine and everything.
Do you think I should dye my hair black?

OUR GUARDIAN ANGELS

Her watery legs led him deeper

Her watery legs led him deeper.

'Alida,' he cried. 'Don't.
I'm supposed to arrest you.'

'Oh yes,' her voice reached back.
'Do you think I chose to be here?'

Her laugh was a child's laugh
at the moment when she is very tired
and about to start crying.

and cheap. Create your own combination of tastes by visiting an assortment of

Waiting for Rick Geary to visit

You never could tell what Mikey was up to.	He had excellent manners but strange hair.	He was often absent from family gatherings.
But he urged his friends to study for their exams.	For his barmitzvah his father bought him an inflatable woman.	Mikey swopped it for a bonsai tree.
His mother considered divorce but he persuaded her against it.	One day a gentile woman came to claim him as her child's father.	Mikey was in the yard learning Xhosa from the maid.
He offered to kill himself but she only wanted a photo for her album.	Mikey decided to go into business.	He exports bonsai marijuana trees to the Far East for aphrodisiac use.

Mikey's motto is: The present is an endless orgasm.
Masitshayisane.

corner cafés (note: these are not sitdown establishments), supermarkets,

THE GIFT SHOP

The angel specialises in wedding lists
for the modern traditional bride.
She has a famous nose for shoplifters.
The cardigan bunched over her wings makes her look lumpy, motherly.

It's nearly closing time, she's cashing up,
one eye on the spatchcock chicken defrosting in her bag,
the other on the last customer
making indecisive gestures near the Tallotti vases.

He looks up, distraught.
'Souvenir? Holiday picture, Sea Point? African lion?'
Where have you been? she asks him.
What have you seen?

Nothing, it turns out, but the hotel conference room.
He's on his way home to Hong Kong tonight.
This was his first time in Africa.
The angel puts down her calculator.

She pushes him out of the shop. It's almost dark.
They warned him about this.
She carries him up the long honeybush road
to the rim of the hill, drags him to the edge,

turns him to face the lights coming on
from Queens Road to Glengariff, the sequin clusters of cars,
the boats at anchor, the lighthouse beam touching the horizon,
takes his camera and photographs him

between the new moon and the evening star,
a pomegranate sunset blazing in his hair,
the South Atlantic Ocean billowing around him like a cape.
She's praying the maid remembered to do potatoes.

Day-old half-price buns and bagels from New York Deli, takeaway coffee from

Sergeant Oliphant
catches himself dreaming

at night.
Walking on the outside of walls
or on rooftops, listening
to the one who thinks of me,
the one who dares not.

From roof to roof casting my net,
sifting your warm dinner smoke
and the starlight hunting your cheeks
where the lashes tremble.

I, the bead in the net
that keeps danger at bay,
the hole in the night
the stars use to reach you

stretched across your dreams, taut as a bowstring
yearning towards its breaking point, waiting.
Whoever cries out will pierce me where I stand
on the lonely horizon, my small grey solitude
disappearing into the hinterland, my swaying step
dragging the ghosts of the cries that have speared me
dream upon dream, so unprotected from my future.

Hey meisie, meisie! I like your style!

Lieg vir my, ek slat jou dood.

Bimbos. Lunch: Many supermarkets offer daily samples of new food items on

HOLIDAY READING

In memory, Jenny

Jenny is there in the dusky kitchen, always
her grey plait and her lovely blue eyes
smiling up at you, and she asks nothing
all day kneeling to clean the soot off the stove, the floor.

On her leg there's a bright abscess, unhealing.
Long ago she ran away from her husband and daughter,
and they brought her back. Now she scours the old pots,
laughing shyly when you visit, turning away.

Still waiting for her tall, dark and handsome one –
she offers you the joke they use for her past.
Her daughter calls you away – oh the sad shame
of the rich child whose mother is poor.

Look, here is the green garden viewed through the sunroom,
a chair with a stool for the leg, a new gown waiting.
But Jenny is still in the kitchen, facing
the man holding her in his secret arms.

In a cream shoebox clean as memory
amber gold eggs are roped together,
and long-stemmed coral and seed pearls,
and blue-eyed Venetian beads studded with starburst roses.
All curled like dancers resting, still warm.

Today her granddaughter will be sent to sell them,
while her daughter leads her into the sunroom, cuts her hair
and the old bandage, binds the leg with clean cotton
and settles her in, where she belongs.

promotion, from mushroom patties to fruitcake. Try Woolworths first. Or splash out

OLD HONEY

His knees ache,
his bones are crumbling inside him,
he's so tired
sweating under his old man's hat
on the balcony, watching
long summer legs stride past
splashing the water up at the bright blue
sky, his eyes hurt
as a memory stirs, just
below his heart, an unfolding step,
a surge, a swirl, he discovers
he's standing in his room
humming something, humming it
over the yellow peaches in the bowl –
the rope of amber beads she wore,
old honey dripping through his fingers
breast warm,
stroking his fingertips –
inside his ribcage a pain melts
through all of him and he sways,
whispering I loved you so
over and over the words fall
from his lips like rope
into the sea
and he can't stop himself
he's smiling, somewhere inside
he's dancing, he remembers what it's like.

on a sliver of parmesan and five marinated olives from Parmigiana. Try their pesto

Stories on a Wednesday night

The trial lawyer almost loses her case
and has a boyfriend who loves her more than his career.
She has a new haircut.

Have you seen this man?
He is wanted in connection with several incidents
of a serious nature.

Tonight the man in the bar
will finally propose to the woman
who always appears briefly in the second half.

There was a drug peddlar
disguised as a scientist. He caused
several teenagers to go crazy and kill themselves.

Is this your number?
If it is you could win half a million rands.
Stay tuned.

In Oslo it's -20°C.
Come to bed. Let's pretend.

Howzit, Clive?
I thought you were in America now.

if at all possible - even on stale bread. Dinner: Samoosas, chili bites, steak pies

LOVE: THE MOVIE

Opening shot: Big Rock. Scene of the action

It heats up under your belly,
the tiny granite specklespikes press through your skin
like fingertips. You feel your back toasting,
the sun fuses your eyelids.

Far away laughter splashes on water.

A wisp of coolness brushes your cheek:
open your eyes: a man's ankles near your lips.
Ice drops sprinkle your shoulders, beckoning.

You roll over the edge.
The water carves your skin open.
Your heart swoops like a swallow on fire.
So
completely
alive.

You're being watched. You sparkle.

Back on the salty towel
steaming gently
you taste the hot clean granite skin
against your mouth.

and koeksisters are filling and sometimes nutritious. Available from all corner

Wide shot: Friends. Not

Susan is happy with anyone. Dates.
Her clothes can't hide her big hips.
She doesn't try. All those boys called Norm and Ivan
laughing like their fathers.

Tanya's found a student.
She's left for First Beach, pseud-cool-dude beach.
I'm fine here
heating up alone, daydreaming
without them and their night plans. Dates.

I'll walk home slowly, as if I'm
trailing sweet memories of love.

Cutaway: Failed experiment. Broken Bath

This friendly beach, they told me. Safe.
When you're sixteen it's hard to tell.
He said Hi, I'm Benny.
Sun-shrivelled, like freckled peach fur.
He made me move my towel three times
saying he'd lost his watch where I lay.
Somewhere in all that sand.

I took a while to cotton on.
His friends all laughing,
lifting their beers as I walked away
trying to look like I had other plans
in my awkward bikini that kept creeping up.

Benny I hope you're reading this. Prat.

shops. Check the sell-by dates. Day 7 Bergie basics Be adventurous - discover

Two-shot: Yes

He's from Joburg. Trust me
to start something that has to end.
Dark. Curly hair. Stunning.
Older than Tanya's student.
He showed me the deepest place to dive
off the back of the Rock.
I don't know what else he'll want me to do.
I'm not too young.

Close-up: I'm

Long hair sun-streaked blonde.
Creamy golden skin glittering with salt.
My blue sarong, white tank top,
stars in my ears, his ankle chain.
This is me. This is me
on Big Rock, tossing my hair in the moonlight.
This is his arm around my shoulders.

This is what it feels like
deep inside. Honey-hot fingers
showering ice.

Freeze frame: The end

They found him under Big Rock
trapped in the kelp garden.

I'm waiting for the detective
to solve the mystery,
fall in love with me,
pull the sun back out of the sea,
and carry me in his strong yet gentle arms
off this rock where I'm stranded.

how the local street survivors make it through the day. Breakfast: Rich pickings

SAFE

Her arm
hung over the railing.

His head was halfway
through the hole in the glass.

They lay like that
all night.

Her taxi driver found them
at dawn, took the money

and left at once,
in case there was trouble.

come from the black bags left outside blocks of flats before 8 am. Borrow a dog to

THE WEDDING WAS AT PADDAVLEI

The frogs burst through the floorboards
in the middle of the ceremony.
It must have been the groom's stamping on the glass
that broke open the hole for them.

Let us remember the Temple that was destroyed
and the exile, the long exile.
The frogs went bananas, leaping
onto everything, ecstatic at the smell of freesias,
the white satin under their cold webby toes,
the red velvet sky wobbling above them.
Or were they insane with shock
after a hundred years buried in lightless mud?
The bride never recovered.

Shit man, I've only got R5.
Just a small one. Come on man!

sniff out meat products efficiently. The higher up the hill you go, the more likely

AT THE END OF THE STORY

Causality and Chance in Love

Chapter 1

His parents
and my parents
caused it all.

That's not true. God, laughing as he turned the page.

Two atoms coughed out
by time's collapsing star.

Libra ascending straight into Scorpio
through Sharpeville, Robben Island and Mowbray.
Arriving in Sea Point
when the law was repealed.

Now we are possible.
Necessary and sufficient conditions.

This happy world that fills our arms.

you are to find leftover French and Italian delicacies. Be sure to give way to the

Chapter 2

Robben Island was more useful
than the little Swiss chalet
with the man and the lady
swinging in and out unreliably
or stuck; the mercury still as a dead ant.

IF YOU SEE	*IT WILL BE*
the clear outline of the island	rain is on the way, and winter winds
a smudge of land in a brown haze	there is dangerous smog in the air
a shimmering blue blur	there will be long and windless heat

*'The healthy colony of penguins
is Robben Island's pride and joy.'*

'I remember the first time all of us heard children's voices in the quarry.
It was as though we had suddenly been struck by lightning. We all stood
dead still, and every one of us was waiting for the moment when we
would glimpse that child. And of course it wasn't allowed. The warders
quickly went and made sure that we didn't actually see the kids. Just
those lone voices – the one occasion in ten years that I actually heard the
voice of a child.'

teams of vagrants sorting the bags into their trolleys; they are often resentful of

Chapter 3

Mist rising on the winter waves
swathed your quarried words in veils
and blew them in to fill my chest with sleeplessness.

I watched the kelp arms of sea creatures reaching through the swell.
You caught the glint of closed windows on the sunlit hills.

Only the wind passing across your lips
and then across my lips, preoccupied with its cargo of rain,
could have imagined us both in the same breath.

Chapter 4

We two waltzing strangely across sand bearing us
tideward, looking over each other's shoulders

at our futures, their lightless eternities
radiating power. Space is curved. We will meet each other

again and again in our pasts that call themselves home,
a little distance from the sunset come to fetch us.

This laughing history that fills our arms.

outsiders. Lunch: Gulls often drop the crusts of toasted sandwiches and chicken

ALIDA AT HOME

Alida at home
never thinks of the sea,
has porcelain lips,
drinks darjeeling tea,
imagines herself
almost happy, quite free.

Her mountaintop walls
grown thick with briar rose
protect her from windcalls
and gullwing shadows.
Woodferns bind the soil
against deep undertows.

Her chandeliers
light mirrored glass.
Inside its frame
moon-edged fins pass
through silent pools
rimmed with black grass.

Her memory moults
in autumn and spring.
Her skin grows smooth,
her cheekbones sing.
Like shells, her ears
keep whispering.

joints they've filched from blue bins near the Wimpy, but can't chew. Rinsed off

AFTERMATH

It's still too hot to sleep.
The wind has died, exhausted,
but flakes of silver trees and mansion plaster
hang in the air, not finished falling.
Fire dust is everywhere in the sealed rooms.

All day the sky was white hot.
Shadows of cautious, darker clouds
were just perceptible behind the tight-lipped sky
that held the heat in.

The night outside looks empty; I imagine
lethargic cockroaches ambling along the gutters,
not particularly hungry.

Somewhere nearby a rumbling air conditioner
reaches its thermostatic peace. Silence
spreads upwards like a breeze.

A new, fine heat starts drifting in behind it.
Small black flies press up against the window,
sucking the dregs of cool air out of the glass
into their papery bellies.

with sea water these are still quite edible. Dinner: Outside the Steer steakhouse and

VIEW

We pay for the view,
enormous sums for the smallest glimpse
of the border.

Shading our eyes from the glare
we stand still, breath held,
scanning this blue country
we are on the edge of, watching
for a sign that we may go home.

The birds dive for fish, laughing,
comparing notes, the ones who've flown in
from Mombasa, the Dakar crowd, the loners
reporting from distant outposts at Omboué, Mtwara, Laâyoune.

We're everywhere, it seems.
Little faces turned to the ocean
like hungry anemones.
And our toes – this is the strangest part –
on mosaic balconies, or oily sand, or carpets
of fishbones and camel dung,
in every place our toes are pushing into the surface,
being sucked in
by some buried current, our uninhabitable past
pulling us back.

Walter's Grill the blue bins fill rapidly with discarded buns, onion rings and bits of

SEAWORTHY

Not retreating
from your cuts and your sores
plastered over,
from your caverns
where rats buy endless rounds of drinks,
from your weeping pavements
and your salt glare,
not shunning the burnt skin
you burnish like shields
and your acid kisses,
not hiding here in my green heart
I am rising,
with my ropes of hunger and my bare feet
I am coming out
to gird you,
your northwest memory
and your southeast curses,
your holds full of golden bones and baby hair,
your raw hull torn through the soil
and filled with seeds,
I am casting my nets
over your glass sails with their arrogant wings,
over your moontrapped mast
and the diamonds stashed in your wicked crow's nest:
holding all your ends together
drawing you close to me,
welding you to my childhood shoulders,
lifting you through the first swell

gristle only partially chewed. Vegans and vegetarians should watch for the

I breast the ocean waiting for us, sure
of your weathered shadow that will be my raft,
and my hand-knotted song, your sounding line:
now we are sailing into the deep century rising under us,
not sinking

late-night cleanouts of soft fruit at the 7-Elevens. Have you tried our new snoek

At the end of the story

The ghosts return at the end of the story.
It's time to go home
but there they sit, having it out
in the invisible room behind unseen walls.
Some kind of meeting.

(Background shadows, those saltwood walls seemed
old crates washed ashore from ancient shipwrecks,
their cargo plundered, the barnacled padlocks closed forever.
Who could have known?)

I found them there, huddled like rotting deckchairs,
counting their grievances off on transparent fingers.
Passing around pictures of their grandchildren –
the members of parliament and TV stars.
Oblivious of the time.

If you hold your ear to the slats
where air has pushed them apart
you can make out the odd phrase:
To be buried in walls we remember.
The granny in the back room.
Something about a publishing contract.

Really, it's time to go home.
But the wind is still full of prowling souls
mad with memory or boredom.
Obviously things aren't over yet.

Who's that walking in my room? Oupa Boeli?

pies? Guaranteed bone-free. Come in for a free taste.

Mind you don't step in it.
Now look what you've done.

NOTES

Page 33, *Klip in die bos*
In summer there are men who make giant tableaux of birds, fish, hearts and love messages out of mussel shells across the sand at Broken Bath beach. People walking on the promenade throw coins down to them.

Page 48, *The RDP comes to Sea Point*
The RDP, or Reconstruction and Development Programme, was a government programme of social welfare initiatives that existed briefly after the election of South Africa's first democratic government in 1994.

Page 59, *Green tin*
The beachfront lawns in Sea Point grow over the landfill of past centuries.

Page 67, *Guess who*
In the 19th century, according to Marischal Murray, Sea Point parents used to invoke two disciplinary forces to make their children behave: Oupa Schaapje, a gentle soul who would bring sweet dreams, and Oupa Boeli, a more malevolent old man who would do nasty things to bad children. Both Oupas were said to walk the streets of Sea Point.

Page 87, *The wedding was at Paddavlei*
The synagogue in Marais Road, Sea Point, is said to be built directly on the site of a marshy frog swamp. The street may have been named for this feature; 'marais' is the French word for marsh.

Page 90, *Causality and chance in love*
The title is adapted from David Bohm's *Causality and Chance in Modern Physics*. From the Sea Point shoreline Robben Island is clearly visible, and has always been a good barometer of forthcoming weather.
Until 1986 the Immorality Act was in force in South Africa – a law forbidding sexual relations between people classified as members of different population groups.

Page 98, *At the end of the story*
Dotted along the promenade between the lawns and the sea are old wooden structures, with no apparent function except as walls against which people can lean or dogs lift their legs.